AIR FRYER COOKBOOK

Guilt-Free, Quick and Easy, Recipes for Your Air Fryer

Louise Davidson

Copyrights

All rights reserved © Louise Davidson and The Cookbook Publisher. No part of this publication or the information in it may be quoted from or reproduced in any form by means such as printing, scanning, photocopying, or otherwise without prior written permission of the copyright holder.

Disclaimer and Terms of Use

Effort has been made to ensure that the information in this book is accurate and complete. However, the author and the publisher do not warrant the accuracy of the information, text, and graphics contained within the book due to the rapidly changing nature of science, research, known and unknown facts, and internet. The author and the publisher do not hold any responsibility for errors, omissions, or contrary interpretation of the subject matter herein. This book is presented solely for motivational and informational purposes only.

The recipes provided in this book are for informational purposes only and are not intended to provide dietary advice. A medical practitioner should be consulted before making any changes in diet. Additionally, recipe cooking times may require adjustment depending on age and quality of appliances. Readers are strongly urged to take all precautions to ensure ingredients are fully cooked in order to avoid the dangers of foodborne illnesses. The recipes and suggestions provided in this book are solely the opinion of the author. The author and publisher do not take any responsibility for any consequences that may result due to following the instructions provided in this book.

ISBN: 978-1542887625

Printed in the United States

Avant-Propos

Are you tired of feeling guilty every time you reach for a French fry or get a craving for spicy chicken wings? You are not alone. There is a new movement, brought on by those who want to be healthy but miss those decadent indulgences, and it all revolves around one simple but amazing appliance: the air fryer. The air fryer "fries" without all the extra oil, making your favorite snacks just as delicious as the originals, but much healthier at the same time. The air fryer, however, is more than a snack food machine. It can help you create an incredible variety of dishes, and this book will help to show you that incredible diversity. From breakfast to dessert and everything in between, this book and your air fryer will get you started on path to healthy eating that is more enjoyable than you ever thought possible.

Happy air frying!

Contents

Introduction 1

  Tips for Using Your Air fryer 2

Breakfast Recipes 5

  Smoked Salmon and Goat Cheese Frittata 5

  Individual Greek Frittatas...6

  Breakfast Empanadas 7

  Old Englishman's Breakfast...9

  Honey Vanilla French Toast with Blackberry Compote 10

Chicken Recipes 11

  Tender Buttermilk Chicken...11

  Smoked Paprika and Cocoa Chicken Breasts 12

  Chicken with Chestnut Stuffing 13

  Chicken Parmesan 15

  Asian Peanut Chicken Skewers 16

  Chipotle Lime Chicken Tenders 17

  Crunchy Honey Mustard Buttermilk Tenders 19

  Jerk Party Wings..21

Pork, Beef and Lamb Recipes 23

  Italian Sausage with Seasoned Roasted Peppers.............23

  "Grilled" Cranberry Ham and Cheese 24

  Pork Chops with Roasted Pepper Mango Salsa 25

  Thai Beef and Rice..27

  Herb Marinated Steak Salad 29

  Italian Beef Rolls..31

  Cajun Rubbed Ribeye Steaks 32

  Lamb Meatballs with Creamy Minted Cucumber Sauce ...33

  Herb Crusted Lamb Chops 35

Fish and Seafood Recipes 37

  Coconut Lime Shrimp 37

  Prosciutto Wrapped Shrimp 38

  Shrimp Spring Rolls 39

  Flakey Fried Whitefish...41

  Cod with Simple Olive Caper Sauce 42

Sesame Soy Striped Bass 43

Garlic Tarragon Buttered Salmon 44

Crab and Herb Croquettes 45

Vegetables, Sides and Snacks 47

Classic French Fries 47

French Fry Style Zucchini..48

Five Spice Eggplant Fries 49

Root Vegetable Snack Chips 50

Mexican Roasted Baby Carrots...51

Brussels Sprouts with Balsamic Shallot Reduction 52

Sweet Potato Croquettes 53

Roasted Caprese Stacks..54

Individual Portabella White Pizzas....................................55

Dessert Recipes 57

Spiced Peach and Pistachio Empanadas..........................57

Walnut Raisin Stuffed Apples..59

Lavender Honey Roasted Figs with Orange Scented Goat
Cheese...60

Papaya Ginger Flan 61

Double Chocolate Brownies 63

Conclusion 65

About the Author 67

More Books from Louise Davidson 68

Appendix – Cooking Conversion Charts 71

Introduction

If you are reading this book, then chances are you are about to enjoy one of the hottest culinary trends today: the air fryer. The air fryer is an amazing appliance that is designed to simplify your life and make you healthier at the same time by taking the guilt out of some of your favorite "fried" foods.

The air fryer works by circulating hot air around the food, and requires very little oil in comparison to traditional fryers. Typically just a small amount of oil is used, and in some cases all you need is a little cooking spray to prevent sticking. Sounds like typical healthy food preparation, right? The bonus is that with the air fryer, you can create crisp French fries, crunchy spring rolls, perfectly fried chicken and more with all the flavor and texture, but with none of the extra calories and fat. As if this wasn't brilliant enough on its own, the air fryer can bake, roast, and steam, making it an indispensible member of your kitchen team.

This book provides you with recipes for delicious "fried" favorites, but it also highlights some of the other healthy cooking styles you can do with your air fryer. You can have your chicken wings, but you can also have tender salmon, melt-in-your-mouth steak, unforgettable side dishes, and even desserts as decadent as flan or rich chocolate brownies. The air fryer is easy to master and the dishes you create will be unforgettably delicious.

Tips for Using Your Air fryer

Preparing to Cook

- For the best finished result, pat off any excess moisture from the foods. This includes meat that has been soaked in a marinade and foods that have a high level of moisture, such as potatoes.
- You need very little oil when you cook with your air fryer, and some food will not require any oil at all. However, if you are not using any oil it is a good idea to use a little non-stick cooking spray applied directly to the food or the basket. This will help prevent your creation from sticking to the basket.
- When cutting an ingredient, try to keep the pieces uniform in size; this will ensure even cooking.
- Double check to make sure any fat drippings have been removed from the bottom of the air fryer after the previous use. Allowing fats and oils to accumulate will cause spattering and create smoke.
- When placing foods in the air fryer, remember to place them so there is plenty of room for air to circulate, even if it means cooking in batches. This will protect the quality of the finished dish and ensure even and proper cooking.
- Preheat the air fryer by setting it to the desired cooking temperature at least three to five minutes before you plan to start cooking.

During Cooking

- Note that recipes and cooking times are an approximation. Your pieces of meat, vegetables, etc. might be a different size or you may wish to alter the amounts of the ingredients. You might also prefer a different level of doneness. Adjust the cooking times up or down depending on the alterations you make, or to suit your individual taste. How closely packed the food is in the air fryer will also impact the amount of time needed for the dish to fully cook.
- Halfway through the cooking time, rotate your food. For smaller items such as fries, this means simply shaking the basket. Larger items should be flipped over.

Always Remember

The air fryer can add an exciting new element to your culinary repertoire. There is no reason you need to stick to traditional "fried" foods. This book will introduce you to additional dishes that can be created in your air fryer. This appliance is meant to be a healthy addition to your kitchen, and with some creativity and experimentation, you can add an incredible variety of fried, roasted, steamed, and baked dishes to your list of culinary creations.

4

Breakfast Recipes
Smoked Salmon and Goat Cheese Frittata

Serves: 4 - Cook Time: 25 minutes
Nutritional Information: Calories 236.0, Total Fat 17.6 g, Saturated Fat 6.8 g,
Total Carbohydrate 2.1 g, Dietary Fiber 0.0 g, Sugars 0.9 g, Protein 16.4 g

Ingredients:
1 tablespoon olive oil
2 tablespoons shallots, diced
6 eggs
1 tablespoon fresh dill
½ teaspoon black pepper
3 tablespoons crème fraîche or heavy cream
1 tablespoon capers
½ cup goat cheese, crumbled
1 cup smoked salmon, flaked or cut into small pieces

Directions:
1. Set the air fryer to 325°F.
2. Place the oil in a skillet over medium heat.
3. Once the oil is hot, add the shallots and sauté until tender.
4. Transfer the shallots into a 6-7 inch pan that can be inserted into the air fryer.
5. In a bowl, combine the eggs, fresh dill, black pepper, and crème fraîche or heavy cream. Whisk the eggs until the yolks are broken up and the mixture is creamy.
6. Sprinkle the smoked salmon, capers, and goat cheese over the onions in the dish.
7. Pour the egg mixture over into the pan.
8. Place the pan in the air fryer and cook for 20 minutes.
9. Serve garnished with additional crème fraîche and dill, if desired.

Individual Greek Frittatas

Serves: 4 - Cook Time: 15-20 minutes
Nutritional Information: Calories 209.8, Total Fat 16.3 g, Saturated Fat 6.1 g,
Total Carbohydrate 4.3 g, Dietary Fiber 1.1 g, Sugars 0.4 g, Protein 11.9 g

Ingredients:
1 tablespoon olive oil
½ cup red onion, diced
2 cloves garlic, crushed and minced
3 cups spinach, torn
6 eggs
2 tablespoons heavy cream
1 teaspoon oregano
½ teaspoon salt
1 teaspoon black pepper
¼ cup black olives, sliced
¼ cup feta cheese, crumbled

Directions:
1. Set the air fryer to 325°F.
2. Heat the olive oil in a skillet over medium heat.
3. Add the red onion and garlic. Sauté for 2-3 minutes.
4. Add the spinach and sauté just until wilted. Remove the skillet from the heat.
5. In a bowl, combine the eggs, heavy cream, oregano, salt, and black pepper. Whisk until the yolks are broken up and the mixture is creamy.
6. Transfer the sautéed vegetables into four individual-sized ramekins.
7. Top the vegetables with sliced olives and feta cheese, followed by the egg mixture.
8. Place the ramekins in the air fryer, working in two batches if necessary.
9. Cook for 10-12 minutes.

Breakfast Empanadas

Serves: 4 - Cook Time: 20 minutes
Nutritional Information: Calories 500.3, Total Fat 30.4 g, Saturated Fat 15.7 g,
Total Carbohydrate 31.9 g, Dietary Fiber 1.8 g, Sugars 0.8 g, Protein 20.5 g

Ingredients:
1 pound crumbled breakfast sausage
½ cup sweet yellow onion, diced
½ cup red bell pepper, diced
1 cup sweet potato, shredded
½ cup cheddar cheese, shredded
½ teaspoon ground sage
½ teaspoon thyme
½ teaspoon salt
1 teaspoon black pepper
1 package prepared empanada shells
1 egg yolk, whisked
Crème fraîche for garnish (optional)

Directions:
1. Set the air fryer to 350°F.
2. Place the breakfast sausage in a skillet over medium heat and cook until thoroughly browned. Drain off the excess grease, leaving about one tablespoon remaining in the skillet.
3. Remove the sausage to a medium mixing bowl, and set it aside.
4. To the skillet add the onion, red bell pepper, and shredded sweet potatoes. Cook, stirring frequently, for 5 minutes or until the vegetables are firm tender.
5. Transfer the vegetables to the bowl with the cooked sausage.
6. Season the mixture with ground sage, fresh thyme, salt, and black pepper and mix.

7. Lay out the empanada shells on a counter or other flat surface.
8. Spoon the sausage mixture onto one half of each of the shells and top with a sprinkling of cheese.
9. Fold each shell in half and crimp it shut with your fingers.
10. Using a fork, press the edges together, ensuring that they are well sealed.
11. Brush each empanada with egg yolk to give it a nice, glossy look when cooked.
12. Place the empanadas in the frying basket and cook for 10-12 minutes.
13. Serve with crème fraîche, if desired.

Old Englishman's Breakfast

Serves: 4 - Cook Time: 20 minutes
Nutritional Information: Calories 294.1, Total Fat 15.1 g, Saturated Fat 5.9 g,
Total Carbohydrate 25.3 g, Dietary Fiber 0.8 g, Sugars 1.0 g, Protein 13.2 g

Ingredients:

1 egg
1 tablespoon vegetable oil
1 cup lamb sausage, cooked and crumbled
¼ cup milk
1 cup flour
1 teaspoon baking powder
1 teaspoon ground sage (optional if using sage derby cheese)
½ teaspoon salt
1 teaspoon black pepper, coarsely ground
½ cup sage derby or white cheddar cheese, shredded
1 teaspoon Worcestershire sauce

Directions:

1. Set the air fryer to 375°F.
2. In a bowl, combine the egg and vegetable oil. Whisk together until blended.
3. Add the lamb sausage and stir.
4. Next, add the milk and blend.
5. Slowly add the flour and baking powder, and season with the ground sage, salt, and black pepper.
6. Finally, stir in the sage derby or white cheddar and Worcestershire sauce.
7. Transfer the mixture to four lightly oiled ramekins.
8. Place the ramekins in the air fryer, working in two batches if necessary.
9. Cook for 20 minutes, or until golden brown.

Honey Vanilla French Toast with Blackberry Compote

Serves: 4 - Cook Time: 10 minutes
Nutritional Information: Calories 233.5, Total Fat 6.5 g, Saturated Fat 2.1 g,
Total Carbohydrate 32.9 g, Dietary Fiber 2.9 g, Sugars 10.4 g, Protein 10.7 g

Ingredients:
1 cup blackberries
¼ cup orange juice
1 teaspoon brown sugar
1 teaspoon allspice
½ teaspoon nutmeg
1 teaspoon lemon zest
4 eggs, beaten
1 teaspoon pure vanilla extract
1 tablespoon local honey
½ teaspoon salt
4 slices thick cut sourdough bread

Directions:
1. In a saucepan, combine the blackberries, orange juice, brown sugar, allspice, nutmeg, and lemon zest. Heat over medium until the liquid bubbles. Reduce the heat to low and simmer, stirring occasionally, until the berries break down and the sauce thickens.
2. Set the air fryer to 350°F.
3. In a bowl, combine the eggs, pure vanilla extract, honey, and salt. Place the bread in a baking dish and pour the egg mixture over it. Turn the bread to make sure both sides are well coated. Let the egg mixture soak in for several minutes.
4. Remove the bread from the bowl and place it in the air fryer.
5. Cook for 6-8 minutes, turning once part way through.
6. Transfer the French toast to serving plates and top it with warm blackberry compote.

Chicken Recipes
Tender Buttermilk Chicken

Serves: 4 - Cook Time: 20 minutes
Nutritional Information: Calories 302.4, Total Fat 6.5 g, Saturated Fat 2.1 g,
Total Carbohydrate 24.7 g, Dietary Fiber 0.7 g, Sugars 7.2 g, Protein 34.3 g

Ingredients:
1 pound boneless, skinless chicken breasts
1 teaspoon paprika
½ teaspoon salt
1 teaspoon black pepper
4 cloves garlic, crushed and minced
1 ½ cups buttermilk
½ cup flour
½ cup panko bread crumbs
2 eggs
2 teaspoons honey

Directions:
1. Place the chicken breasts in a large bowl and season them with the paprika, salt, and black pepper.
2. Sprinkle the crushed garlic over the chicken and add the buttermilk. Cover and refrigerate for at least 12 hours.
3. Set the air fryer to 375°F.
4. In one bowl, combine the flour and panko bread crumbs.
5. In a separate bowl, whisk together the egg and honey.
6. Remove the chicken from the marinade.
7. Dredge each piece of chicken through the flour mixture, then dip it in the egg mixture and once again into the flour mixture.
8. Place the chicken breasts in the air fryer and cook for 20-22 minutes, or until the chicken is cooked through.

Smoked Paprika and Cocoa Chicken Breasts

Serves: 4 - Cook Time: 20 minutes
Nutritional Information: Calories 278.1, Total Fat 4.0 g, Saturated Fat 1.3 g,
Total Carbohydrate 27.3 g, Dietary Fiber 1.1 g, Sugars 3.3 g, Protein 31.1 g

Ingredients:

4 boneless, skinless chicken breasts
1 cup milk
1 cup flour
½ teaspoon salt
1 teaspoon black pepper, coarsely ground
1 teaspoon smoked paprika
1 teaspoon garlic powder
½ teaspoon cayenne powder
½ teaspoon coriander
2 teaspoons cocoa powder

Directions:

1. Set the air fryer to 375°F.
2. Place the chicken breasts in a shallow baking dish and cover them with the milk. Let them sit for at least 5 minutes.
3. Meanwhile, combine the flour with the salt, black pepper, smoked paprika, garlic powder, cayenne powder, coriander, and cocoa powder. Mix well.
4. Remove the chicken from the milk and shake off any excess.
5. Dredge each piece of chicken through the spiced flour mixture.
6. Place the chicken breasts in the air fryer and cook for 20-22 minutes, or until cooked through.

Chicken with Chestnut Stuffing

Serves: 4 - Cook Time: 50 minutes
Nutritional Information: Calories 340.1, Total Fat 13.1 g, Saturated Fat 5.1 g,
Total Carbohydrate 38.4 g, Dietary Fiber 2.7 g, Sugars 0.6 g, Protein 16.9 g

Ingredients:
2 tablespoons butter
1 cup yellow onion, diced
1 cup celery, diced
1 tablespoon dried sage
1 tablespoon dried thyme
1 ½ cups chestnuts, chopped and roasted
4 cups sourdough bread pieces, torn and toasted
½ cup chicken stock (adjust to preference)
1 whole chicken, approximately 2 ½–3 pounds
1 tablespoon olive oil
1 teaspoon salt
1 teaspoon black pepper

Directions:
1. Place the butter in a skillet over medium heat.
2. Once the butter has melted, add the onion and celery. Sauté for 2-3 minutes.
3. Season the vegetables with the sage and thyme and add the chestnuts.
4. Cook, stirring frequently, for 5 minutes.
5. Add the bread and toss. Slowly add the chicken stock until the bread cubes are moistened according to your personal preference.
6. Remove the skillet from the heat, and set it aside.
7. Set the air fryer to 390°F.
8. Remove any innards from the chicken and spoon the chestnut stuffing onto the center of a piece of cheesecloth.

9. Tie the cheesecloth and place it inside the chicken.
10. Brush the chicken with olive oil and season it with salt and black pepper.
11. Place the chicken in the air fryer and cook for 40 minutes, or until the chicken is cooked through.
12. Remove the chicken from the fryer and remove the stuffing from the cavity.
13. Place the stuffing in a microwave safe dish.
14. Let the chicken rest for 5 minutes.
15. While the chicken is resting, microwave the stuffing for 3-4 minutes, or until a food thermometer reads at least 145° when inserted into the middle.
16. Serve the chicken with the stuffing on the side.

Chicken Parmesan

Serves: 4 - Cook Time: 10 minutes
Nutritional Information: Calories 450.9, Total Fat 17.3 g, Saturated Fat 8.6 g,
Total Carbohydrate 29.6 g, Dietary Fiber 2.4 g, Sugars 4.6 g, Protein 42.5 g

Ingredients:

½ cup flour
1 teaspoon salt
1 teaspoon black pepper
1 cup panko bread crumbs
½ cup Asiago cheese, freshly grated
¼ cup fresh basil, chopped
1 teaspoon lemon zest
4 boneless, skinless chicken breasts, pounded thin
2 teaspoons olive oil
1 egg, beaten
1 cup marinara sauce, warmed
½ cup fresh mozzarella, sliced
Cooked pasta for serving, optional

Directions:

1. Set the air fryer to 375°F.
2. In one bowl, combine the flour with the salt and black pepper.
3. In another bowl, combine the panko bread crumbs with the grated Asiago cheese, fresh basil, and lemon zest.
4. Lightly brush each piece of chicken with olive oil.
5. Dredge each piece of chicken through the flour mixture.
6. Next, dip each piece of chicken into the beaten egg and then dredge it through the bread crumb mixture.
7. Place the pieces of chicken in the air fryer and cook for 6-8 minutes, until browned and cooked through.
8. Place the chicken over pasta, if desired, and top with marinara sauce and fresh sliced mozzarella.

Asian Peanut Chicken Skewers

Serves: 4 - Cook Time: 10 minutes
Nutritional Information: Calories 451.9, Total Fat 29.3 g, Saturated Fat 5.7 g,
Total Carbohydrate 12.7 g, Dietary Fiber 2.3 g, Sugars 7.8 g, Protein 34.8 g

Ingredients:
½ cup creamy peanut butter
½ cup low sodium soy sauce
½ cup pineapple juice
3 tablespoons sesame oil
1 tablespoon jalapeño pepper, diced
2 cloves garlic, crushed and minced
2 teaspoons fresh ginger, grated
½ teaspoon cayenne powder
½ teaspoon black pepper
1 pound chicken tenders
¼ cup fresh cilantro, chopped
Cooked rice for serving, optional

Directions:
1. In a bowl, combine the creamy peanut butter, soy sauce, pineapple juice, and sesame oil. Whisk together until combined.
2. Add the jalapeño pepper, garlic, ginger, cayenne powder, and black pepper. Mix well.
3. Thread each chicken tender on a bamboo skewer.
4. Place the skewers in a shallow baking dish.
5. Pour the sauce over the chicken and turn it to make sure both sides are evenly coated.
6. Cover and place the dish in the refrigerator for at least 2 hours.
7. Set the air fryer to 390°F.
8. Remove the skewers from the marinade and place them in the air fryer basket.
9. Cook for 7-8 minutes, or until cooked through.
10. Garnish with fresh cilantro and serve with cooked rice, if desired.

Chipotle Lime Chicken Tenders

Serves: 4 - Cook Time: 10 minutes
Nutritional Information: Calories 362.6, Total Fat 8.8 g, Saturated Fat 1.7 g,
Total Carbohydrate 36.8 g, Dietary Fiber 1.1 g, Sugars 5.1 g, Protein 31.9 g

Ingredients:

½ cup chipotle peppers in adobo sauce

1 tablespoon lime juice

1 tablespoon honey

1 pound chicken tenders

1 cup flour

1 teaspoon salt

1 teaspoon black pepper

1 teaspoon garlic powder

1 cup panko bread crumbs

1 teaspoon lime zest

1 tablespoon olive oil

2 eggs, beaten

Directions:

1. In a bowl, combine the chipotle peppers in adobo sauce with the lime juice and honey. Mix well.
2. Place the chicken tenders in a shallow baking dish and pour in the chipotle sauce. Turn the chicken to make sure both sides are evenly coated.
3. Let the chicken marinate for 15 minutes, or cover and refrigerate for up to 12 hours.
4. Set the air fryer to 390°F.
5. In a bowl, combine the flour, salt, black pepper, and garlic powder.
6. In a separate bowl, combine the panko bread crumbs, lime zest, and olive oil. Mix well.
7. Remove the chicken tenders from the marinade and dredge them lightly in the seasoned flour.

8. Next, lightly coat each tender with the beaten egg and dredge it through the bread crumb mixture. Pat the bread crumbs on to make sure they stick.
9. Place the chicken tenders in the basket of the air fryer and cook for approximately 10 minutes, turning once halfway through, or until the chicken is cooked through.

Crunchy Honey Mustard Buttermilk Tenders

Serves: 4 - Cook Time: 10 minutes
Nutritional Information: Calories 382.0, Total Fat 8.7 g, Saturated Fat 2.1 g,
Total Carbohydrate 37.2 g, Dietary Fiber 1.1 g, Sugars 7.9 g, Protein 33.3 g

Ingredients:

1 pound chicken tenders
1 cup buttermilk
¼ cup Dijon mustard
2 tablespoons local honey
1 cup flour
1 teaspoon salt
1 teaspoon black pepper
1 teaspoon mustard powder
2 eggs, beaten
1 cup panko bread crumbs
1 tablespoon fresh thyme, chopped
1 tablespoon olive oil

Directions:

1. Place the chicken tenders in a shallow baking dish.
2. In a bowl, combine the buttermilk, Dijon mustard, and local honey. Whisk until well combined.
3. Pour the buttermilk mixture over the chicken tenders. Turn the chicken to make sure it is evenly coated.
4. Cover the dish and place it in the refrigerator for 2 hours.
5. Set the air fryer to 390°F.
6. In one bowl, combine the flour with the salt, black pepper, and mustard powder.
7. In a separate bowl, combine the panko bread crumbs, fresh thyme, and olive oil. Mix well.
8. Remove the chicken from the buttermilk marinade and shake off any extra liquid.

9. Coat the chicken tenders in the flour mixture then dip them into the beaten egg.
10. Next, place the chicken tenders in the panko mixture and pat the crumbs onto each one, making sure they stick.
11. Place the chicken tenders in the basket of the air fryer.
12. Cook for approximately 10 minutes, turning once halfway through, until the chicken is cooked through.

Jerk Party Wings

Serves: 6 - Cook Time: 15 minutes
Nutritional Information: Calories 324.6, Total Fat 23.7 g, Saturated Fat 6.3 g,
Total Carbohydrate 2.8 g, Dietary Fiber 0.1 g, Sugars 2.2 g, Protein 26.0 g

Ingredients:
1 tablespoon olive oil
4 cloves garlic, crushed and minced
1 jalapeño pepper, diced
½ teaspoon cayenne powder
2 teaspoons allspice
1 teaspoon cinnamon
½ teaspoon ground ginger
1 teaspoon black pepper, coarsely ground
¼ cup soy sauce
1 tablespoon garlic chili paste
1 tablespoon brown sugar
2 tablespoons lime juice
2 pounds chicken wings

Directions:
1. Set the air fryer to 390°F.
2. In a bowl, combine the olive oil, garlic, jalapeño pepper, cayenne powder, allspice, cinnamon, ground ginger, and black pepper. Mix well.
3. To the seasoned olive oil add the soy sauce, garlic chili paste, brown sugar, and lime juice. Whisk together until blended.
4. Place the chicken wings in a shallow baking dish and pour the marinade over the wings.
5. Let the chicken marinate for at least 20 minutes, or up to 2 hours.
6. Remove the chicken from the marinade and place it in the basket of the air fryer.
7. Cook for approximately 15 minutes, or until the wings are cooked through.

22

Pork, Beef and Lamb Recipes
Italian Sausage with Seasoned Roasted Peppers

Serves: 4 - Cook Time: 15 minutes
Nutritional Information: Calories 381.7, Total Fat 26.9 g, Saturated Fat 13.3 g, Total Carbohydrate 16.1 g, Dietary Fiber 3.2 g, Sugars 3.0 g, Protein 18.2 g

Ingredients:
1 pound Italian sausage
2 cups green bell pepper, cut into thick slices
2 cups red bell pepper, cut into thick slices
1 cup yellow bell pepper, cut into thick slices
2 cups sweet yellow onion, cut into thick slices
1 tablespoon olive oil
¼ cup fresh basil
1 tablespoon fresh oregano
½ teaspoon salt
1 teaspoon black pepper

Directions:
1. Set the air fryer to 390°F.
2. Combine the green, red, and yellow bell peppers with the sweet yellow onion in a large bowl or on a baking sheet.
3. Drizzle the vegetables with olive oil, and season with basil, oregano, salt, and pepper. Toss to coat.
4. Place the vegetables in the basket of the air fryer and cook for 3-4 minutes. Remove and set them aside.
5. Reduce the heat of the air fryer to 375°F.
6. Place the sausages in the air fryer and cook for 10 minutes, or until cooked through.
7. Serve the sausages on a bed of the seasoned roasted peppers

"Grilled" Cranberry Ham and Cheese

Serves: 4 - Cook Time: 5 minutes
Nutritional Information: Calories 473.0, Total Fat 17.1 g, Saturated Fat 9.3 g,
Total Carbohydrate 53.8 g, Dietary Fiber 2.2 g, Sugars 12.7 g, Protein 23.0 g

Ingredients:

8 slices sourdough bread (or preferred bread)
2 tablespoons butter, melted
1 tablespoon Dijon mustard
¼ cup cranberry sauce
½ pound smoked ham, shaved
¼ cup Brie cheese, sliced
½ cup Gruyere cheese, shredded
1 cup arugula leaves

Directions:

1. Set the air fryer to 355°F.
2. Lay the bread out on a counter or clean surface. Liberally brush the butter over one side of each piece, and then flip the bread over.
3. On four of the slices, apply the Dijon mustard and cranberry sauce.
4. Follow by placing the ham, Brie, Gruyere, and arugula on the bread.
5. Top each with an additional piece of bread.
6. Working in batches, place the sandwiches into the air fryer and cook for 5 minutes.

Pork Chops with Roasted Pepper Mango Salsa

Serves: 4 - Cook Time: 15 minutes
Nutritional Information: Calories 274.1, Total Fat 15.7 g, Saturated Fat 3.5 g,
Total Carbohydrate 10.3 g, Dietary Fiber 1.1 g, Sugars 9.0 g, Protein 21.4 g

Ingredients:

¼ cup olive oil

2 tablespoons pineapple juice

2 cloves garlic, crushed and minced

1 tablespoon fresh mint, divided

2 tablespoons fresh cilantro, chopped and divided

1 tablespoon Dijon mustard

1 sprig fresh rosemary

1 pound pork chops, approximately 1 inch thick

1-2 jalapeño peppers, depending upon heat preference

1 red bell pepper, whole

1 cup mango, chopped

½ teaspoon salt

½ teaspoon pepper

½ teaspoon cumin

½ teaspoon coriander

Directions:

1. In a bowl, combine the olive oil, pineapple juice, garlic, mint, 1 tablespoon of the cilantro, Dijon mustard, and rosemary.
2. Place the pork chops in a shallow baking dish and cover them with the marinade.
3. Cover and refrigerate for 2 hours.
4. Remove the pork chops from the refrigerator and let them sit at room temperature for 15 minutes.
5. Set the air fryer to 390°F.

6. Place the jalapeño peppers and red pepper in the basket of the air fryer and cook for 3 minutes.
7. Remove the peppers from the air fryer and place them in a bowl. Cover the bowl with plastic wrap and let the peppers sweat for 5-10 minutes.
8. Remove the peppers from the bowl, peel away the skin, and dice.
9. Combine the diced peppers with the mango, salt, pepper, cumin, coriander, and remaining cilantro. Mix well and set aside.
10. Set the air fryer to 390°F again.
11. Place the pork chops in the basket, working in batches if necessary.
12. Cook for approximately 10 minutes, or until cooked through.
13. Serve with the fresh mango salsa.

Thai Beef and Rice

Serves: 8 - Cook Time: 40 minutes
Nutritional Information: Calories 584.7, Total Fat 32.2 g, Saturated Fat 3.2 g,
Total Carbohydrate 35.2 g, Dietary Fiber 2.8 g, Sugars 0.2 g, Protein 36.5 g

Ingredients:

1 beef roast, approximately 2 pounds
¼ cup olive oil
¼ cup low sodium soy sauce
¼ cup fish sauce
2 tablespoons lime juice
1 tablespoon sesame oil
¼ cup beef stock
1 habanero pepper, diced
3 cloves garlic, crushed and minced
¼ cup red onion, diced
1 tablespoon fresh ginger, grated
½ teaspoon salt
1 teaspoon black pepper, coarsely ground
6 cups cooked rice for serving

Directions:

1. Place the roast in a bowl or shallow baking dish.
2. In a separate bowl, combine the olive oil, soy sauce, fish sauce, lime juice, sesame oil, beef stock, habanero pepper, garlic, red onion, ginger, salt, and black pepper. Mix well.
3. Cover the roast with the marinade.
4. Place the roast in the refrigerator for at least 2 hours, turning once halfway through to make sure all of it is marinated equally.
5. Set the air fryer to 390°F.
6. Place the roast in the air fryer and cook for 40 minutes for medium rare, or until the desired doneness is reached.

7. Remove the roast from the air fryer and let it rest 10 minutes.
8. Slice the roast into thin pieces and serve it over hot, cooked rice.

Herb Marinated Steak Salad

Serves: 4 - Cook Time: 15 minutes
Nutritional Information: Calories 455.1, Total Fat 35.6 g, Saturated Fat 7.3 g,
Total Carbohydrate 9.3 g, Dietary Fiber 3.3 g, Sugars 3.0 g, Protein 24.8 g

Ingredients:

1 pound flank steak, cut into 4-5 pieces
½ cup olive oil
¼ cup balsamic vinegar
1 cup fresh parsley, chopped
¼ cup fresh cilantro, chopped
¼ cup fresh mint, chopped
1 tablespoon fresh tarragon
4 cloves garlic, crushed and minced
½ teaspoon cayenne powder
1 teaspoon paprika
1 teaspoon salt
1 teaspoon black pepper
6 cups mixed salad greens
1 cup roasted red peppers, sliced
1 cup portabella mushrooms, sliced
1 cup canned artichoke hearts, quartered

Directions:

1. Place the steak pieces in a shallow baking dish.
2. In a blender or food processor, combine the olive oil, balsamic vinegar, parsley, cilantro, mint, tarragon, garlic, cayenne powder, paprika, salt, and black pepper. Blend until combined.
3. Coat the steak with about half of the marinade mixture. Reserve the rest to garnish the salad.
4. Cover the steak and marinate for at least 4 hours or overnight.
5. Set the air fryer to 390°F.

6. Remove the steak from the marinade and place it in the air fryer. Cook for 10-12 minutes, depending upon desired doneness.
7. While the steak is cooking, combine the mixed salad greens, roasted red peppers, portabella mushrooms, and canned artichoke hearts, and arrange the salad on individual serving plates.
8. Remove the steak from the air fryer and let it rest at least 5 minutes before slicing it into thin strips.
9. Place the strips of steak over the salad and garnish with a drizzle of the prepared herb sauce.

Italian Beef Rolls

Serves: 6 - Cook Time: 15 minutes
Nutritional Information: Calories 277.7, Total Fat 15.9 g, Saturated Fat 6.2 g,
Total Carbohydrate 3.1 g, Dietary Fiber 0.7 g, Sugars 1.2 g, Protein 29.5 g

Ingredients:
1 cup fresh basil
1 cup fresh parsley
¼ cup pine nuts
2 cloves garlic
1 teaspoon lemon zest
½ teaspoon salt
½ teaspoon black pepper
¼ cup Parmesan cheese, freshly grated
3 tablespoons olive oil
1 ½ pounds flank steak, butterfly cut
1 cup fresh mozzarella cheese, sliced
1 cup fresh spinach, torn
1 cup roasted red peppers, sliced

Directions:
1. In a blender or food processor combine the basil, parsley, pine nuts, garlic, lemon zest, salt, black pepper, Parmesan, and olive oil. Pulse until well blended.
2. Lay the steak out on the counter and open up the butterfly cut.
3. Spread the herb sauce over the steak.
4. Next, layer on the mozzarella cheese, spinach, and roasted red bell peppers.
5. Roll the steak up and secure it with cooking twine or toothpicks throughout.
6. Set the air fryer to 400°F.
7. Place the steak roll in the air fryer and cook for 15 minutes, or until the desired doneness is reached.
8. Remove the steak roll from the air fryer and let it rest for 10 minutes before removing the twine or toothpicks and slicing.

Cajun Rubbed Ribeye Steaks

Serves: 4 - Cook Time: 15 minutes
Nutritional Information: Calories 358.0, Total Fat 15.5 g, Saturated Fat 4.5 g,
Total Carbohydrate 0.0 g, Dietary Fiber 0.0 g, Sugars 0.0 g, Protein 50.0 g

Ingredients:

1 tablespoon Cajun seasoning
1 teaspoon black pepper, coarsely ground
1 teaspoon garlic powder
1 teaspoon powdered ground coffee
1 tablespoon olive oil
1 ½ pounds ribeye steaks

Directions:

1. Set the air fryer to 400°F.
2. Combine the Cajun seasoning, black pepper, garlic powder, and powdered ground coffee.
3. Add the olive oil to the spice mixture and combine until a paste forms.
4. Rub both sides of each steak with the Cajun spice paste.
5. Place the steaks in the basket of the air fryer and cook for 15 minutes, adjusting for desired doneness. Turn once halfway through cooking.
6. Remove the steaks from the air fryer and let them rest for 10 minutes before serving.

Lamb Meatballs with Creamy Minted Cucumber Sauce

Serves: 4 - Cook Time: 15 minutes
Nutritional Information: Calories 482.8, Total Fat 39.7 g, Saturated Fat 15.5 g,
Total Carbohydrate 2.8 g, Dietary Fiber 0.0 g, Sugars 2.2 g, Protein 27.8 g

Ingredients:

1 pound ground lamb

¼ pound ground chicken or turkey

1 egg

3 cloves garlic, crushed and minced

2 teaspoons crushed red pepper flakes

1 teaspoon ground cumin

1 teaspoon coriander

1 teaspoon salt

1 teaspoon black pepper

1 tablespoon fresh mint, chopped

2 tablespoons fresh parsley, chopped

1 tablespoon harissa

2 tablespoons olive oil

For the Sauce

½ cup plain Greek yogurt

¼ cup sour cream or crème fraîche

2 cloves garlic, crushed and minced

½ cup cucumber, peeled and finely chopped

¼ cup fresh mint, chopped

1 teaspoon garam masala

1 tablespoon lime juice

½ teaspoon salt

Directions:

1. Before making the meatballs, combine all the ingredients for the sauce. Mix well and set aside, or cover and refrigerate until ready to use.
2. Set the air fryer to 390°F.
3. In a bowl, combine the ground lamb, ground turkey, and egg. Gently mix using your hands.
4. Next, season the mixture with the garlic, crushed red pepper flakes, cumin, coriander, salt, pepper, mint, parsley, harissa, and olive oil. Mix well.
5. Using your hands, take heaping spoonfuls of the meat mixture and form golf ball sized meatballs.
6. Place the meatballs in the basket of the air fryer, leaving some space between them.
7. Cook, working in batches if necessary, for 7-8 minutes, or until cooked through.
8. Remove the meatballs from the air fryer.
9. Place a spoonful of the cucumber sauce on serving plates and top with the meatballs.

Herb Crusted Lamb Chops

Serves: 4 - Cook Time: 10 minutes
Nutritional Information: Calories 306.6, Total Fat 13.5 g, Saturated Fat 4.8 g,
Total Carbohydrate 6.6 g, Dietary Fiber 0.3 g, Sugars 0.5 g, Protein 37.6 g

Ingredients:

1 ½ pounds lamb chops
½ teaspoon salt
½ teaspoon black pepper
1 tablespoon fresh tarragon, chopped
1 tablespoon fresh mint, chopped
1 tablespoon fresh parsley, chopped
1 tablespoon shallots, finely diced
1 teaspoon lemon zest, freshly grated
¼ cup Parmesan cheese, freshly grated
½ cup panko bread crumbs
1 tablespoon Dijon mustard
1 tablespoon olive oil

Directions:

1. Set the air fryer to 390°F.
2. Season the lamb chops with salt and black pepper.
3. In a blender or food processor, combine the tarragon, mint, parsley, shallots, lemon zest, Parmesan cheese, and panko bread crumbs. Pulse until well blended.
4. Add the Dijon mustard and olive oil and mix well.
5. Spread the herb mixture on both sides of each of the lamb chops.
6. Place the lamb chops in the basket of the air fryer.
7. Cook for 10-12 minutes, or until the desired doneness is reached.
8. Remove the chops to a platter, and let them rest for at least 5 minutes before serving.

36

Fish and Seafood Recipes
Coconut Lime Shrimp

Serves: 4 - Cook Time: 10 minutes
Nutritional Information: Calories 350.3, Total Fat 12.3 g, Saturated Fat 9.4 g,
Total Carbohydrate 31.9 g, Dietary Fiber 2.9 g, Sugars 1.1 g, Protein 28.1 g

Ingredients:
1 pound shrimp, cleaned and deveined
1 cup unsweetened, shredded coconut
1 tablespoon lime zest, grated
½ teaspoon cayenne powder
1 cup flour
1 tablespoon cornstarch
1 teaspoon salt
1 teaspoon pepper
1 egg white

Directions:
1. Set the air fryer to 350°F.
2. In a bowl, combine the unsweetened shredded coconut, lime zest, and cayenne powder.
3. In a second bowl, combine the flour, cornstarch, salt, and pepper.
4. Place the egg white in a third bowl.
5. One at a time, dip each shrimp first in the flour mixture, then the egg white, and then in the coconut mixture, patting on the coconut with your fingers to make sure it sticks.
6. Place the shrimp in the basket of the air fryer.
7. Cook for 10 minutes, turning once halfway through.

Prosciutto Wrapped Shrimp

Serves: 4 - Cook Time: 10 minutes
Nutritional Information: Calories 260.1, Total Fat 12.0 g, Saturated Fat 4.4 g,
Total Carbohydrate 3.0 g, Dietary Fiber 0.0 g, Sugars 0.0 g, Protein 34.0 g

Ingredients:

1 pound shrimp, cleaned and deveined
2 teaspoons lemon juice
½ teaspoon salt
1 teaspoon black pepper
½ teaspoon garlic powder
½ pound prosciutto, or enough to wrap each shrimp with one
piece

Directions:

1. Set the air fryer to 350°F.
2. Season the shrimp with the lemon juice, salt, black pepper, and garlic powder.
3. Take one piece of prosciutto and wrap it completely around one piece of shrimp.
4. Repeat until all the shrimp is wrapped, and place it in the basket of the air fryer.
5. Cook for 10 minutes, or until the shrimp is cooked all the way through.

Shrimp Spring Rolls

Serves: 4 - Cook Time: 15 minutes
Nutritional Information: Calories 172.9, Total Fat 5.1 g, Saturated Fat 0.8 g.
Total Carbohydrate 24.5 g, Dietary Fiber 1.3 g, Sugars 20.8 g, Protein 6.7 g

Ingredients:
1 tablespoon peanut oil
1 teaspoon sesame oil
2 cloves garlic, crushed and minced
1 teaspoon fresh ginger, grated
¼ cup water chestnuts, cut into small strips
½ cup carrots, shredded
½ cup cabbage, shredded
¼ cup scallions, sliced
1 tablespoon soy sauce
1 teaspoon five spice powder
1 teaspoon salt
1 teaspoon pepper
¼ pound shrimp, cleaned, deveined and sliced
½ cup bean sprouts
12-14 spring roll wrappers
1 egg, lightly beaten

Directions:
1. Heat the peanut oil and sesame oil in a large skillet over medium heat.
2. Add the garlic, ginger, chestnuts, carrots, cabbage, scallions, and soy sauce.
3. Season the mixture with five spice powder, salt, and pepper. Sauté the mixture for 3-5 minutes.
4. Add the shrimp and bean sprouts. Cook just until the shrimp is pink, and then remove the skillet from the heat.
5. Lay the spring roll wrappers out on the counter or other flat surface.

6. Brush the ends with the beaten egg mixture.
7. Place a generous spoonful of the mixture onto each spring roll wrapper.
8. Roll each one up, fold in the ends, and press the edge to seal.
9. Lightly brush the spring roll with the egg mixture again, if desired.
10. Set the air fryer to 390°F.
11. Place the spring rolls in the basket of the air fryer and cook for 5 minutes.
12. Serve with your favorite dipping sauce, if desired.

Flakey Fried Whitefish

Serves: 4 - Cook Time: 15 minutes
Nutritional Information: Calories 372.8, Total Fat 14.8 g, Saturated Fat 2.6 g,
Total Carbohydrate 24.1 g, Dietary Fiber 0.9 g, Sugars 1.1 g, Protein 34.0 g

Ingredients:

1 pound whitefish fillets, cut into 3-4 inch pieces
2 teaspoons fresh lemon juice
1 teaspoon salt
1 teaspoon black pepper
½ cup flour
2 eggs, lightly beaten
1 cup panko bread crumbs
1 tablespoon fresh tarragon, chopped
1 tablespoon fresh parsley chopped
1 tablespoon olive oil

Directions:

1. Set the air fryer to 390°F.
2. Sprinkle the whitefish fillets with lemon juice and season them with salt and black pepper.
3. Place the flour in one bowl and the eggs in a second bowl.
4. In a third bowl, combine the panko bread crumbs, tarragon, parsley, and olive oil. Mix until the olive oil is worked through the crumbs.
5. Dust a piece of whitefish with the flour, and then dip it into the egg mixture.
6. Next, place it into the panko mixture and use your hands to pat the crumbs onto the fish. Repeat until all the pieces are coated.
7. Place the whitefish pieces in the basket of the air fryer.
8. Cook for 12-15 minutes, or until the fish is cooked through.

Cod with Simple Olive Caper Sauce

Serves: 4 - Cook Time: 15 minutes
Nutritional Information: Calories 164.7, Total Fat 5.2 g, Saturated Fat 0.8 g,
Total Carbohydrate 2.2 g, Dietary Fiber 0.8 g, Sugars 1.0 g, Protein 25.7 g

Ingredients:
1 pound cod pieces
1 tablespoon plus 1 teaspoon olive oil
1 teaspoon lemon juice
1 teaspoon salt
1 teaspoon black pepper
1 cup cherry tomatoes, halved
2 cloves garlic, crushed and minced
¼ cup Kalamata olives, diced
1 tablespoon capers
¼ cup fresh basil, chopped

Directions:
1. Set the air fryer to 355°F.
2. Lightly brush the cod with 1 teaspoon of the olive oil.
3. Sprinkle the cod with lemon juice and season it with salt and black pepper.
4. Place the cod in the basket of the air fryer.
5. Cook for 12 minutes, or until the cod is flakey and tender.
6. While the cod is cooking, heat the remaining olive oil in a large skillet over medium.
7. Add the tomatoes and cook for 2-3 minutes, or until they begin to break down and release their juices.
8. Next, add the garlic, olives, capers, and basil to the skillet. Cook, stirring frequently, for 4-5 minutes.
9. Remove the cod from the air fryer and transfer it to serving plates.
10. Top the cod with the olive caper sauce before serving.

Sesame Soy Striped Bass

Serves: 4 - Cook Time: 10 minutes
Nutritional Information: Calories 311.0, Total Fat 10.2 g, Saturated Fat 1.7 g,
Total Carbohydrate 23.1 g, Dietary Fiber 0.5 g, Sugars 18.3 g, Protein 29.8 g

Ingredients:

1 pound striped bass steaks
1 cup soy sauce
½ cup mirin
2 tablespoons sesame oil
2 tablespoons brown sugar
1 tablespoon lime juice
1 tablespoon garlic chili paste
¼ cup apple juice

Directions:

1. Place the bass steaks in a shallow baking dish.
2. In a bowl, combine the soy sauce, mirin, sesame oil, brown sugar, lime juice, garlic chili paste, and apple juice. Use a whisk to blend.
3. Cover the steaks with the sesame soy sauce, cover, and refrigerate for one hour.
4. Set the air fryer to 390°F.
5. Remove the bass from the marinade and blot up any extra.
6. Place the steaks in the air fryer and cook for approximately 10 minutes, or until the fish is cooked through and flakey.
7. Remove the bass from the air fryer and let it rest several minutes before serving.

Garlic Tarragon Buttered Salmon

Serves: 4 - Cook Time: 20 minutes
Nutritional Information: Calories 272.6, Total Fat 16.5 g, Saturated Fat 8.1 g,
Total Carbohydrate 0.4 g, Dietary Fiber 0.0 g, Sugars 0.0 g, Protein 29.1 g

Ingredients:
¼ cup butter
1 tablespoon shallot, diced
1 tablespoon fresh tarragon, chopped
1 teaspoon fresh lemon zest
1 pound salmon fillets
1 teaspoon salt
1 teaspoon black pepper
Fresh lemon slices for garnish

Directions:
1. Set the air fryer to 350°F.
2. Melt the butter in a saucepan over medium heat.
3. Once the butter has melted, add the shallot, tarragon, and lemon zest. Cook, stirring frequently, for 2-3 minutes. Remove it from the heat and set it aside.
4. Season the salmon fillets with salt and black pepper.
5. Liberally brush both sides of each piece of salmon with the garlic tarragon butter.
6. Place the salmon pieces in the air fryer and cook for 15 minutes, turning once halfway through.
7. Remove the salmon from the air fryer and garnish with any remaining butter sauce and fresh lemon slices.

Crab and Herb Croquettes

Serves: 4 - Cook Time: 15 minutes
Nutritional Information: Calories 339.4, Total Fat 10.3 g, Saturated Fat 3.1 g,
Total Carbohydrate 28.3 g, Dietary Fiber 1.5 g, Sugars 1.4 g, Protein 32.3 g

Ingredients:

1 tablespoon olive oil
½ cup red onion, diced
¼ cup celery, diced
¼ cup red bell pepper, diced
3 cloves garlic, crushed and minced
1 teaspoon salt
1 teaspoon black pepper
1 tablespoon fresh tarragon, chopped
1 tablespoon fresh parsley, chopped
1 pound lump crab meat, shredded
¼ cup sour cream
2 eggs
½ cup flour
1 cup panko bread crumbs
1 teaspoon fresh lemon zest
1-2 teaspoon crushed red pepper flakes

Directions:

1. Place the olive oil in a skillet over medium heat.
2. Add the red onion, celery, red bell pepper, and garlic. Cook, stirring frequently, for approximately 5 minutes, or until the vegetables begin to become tender.
3. Season the mixture with salt, black pepper, tarragon, and parsley. Remove the skillet from the heat and allow it to cool enough so the mixture can be handled.
4. Next, transfer the vegetables to a bowl and add the lump crab meat, sour cream, and 1 egg. Mix well.
5. Set the air fryer to 390°F.

6. Place the flour in a bowl. In a second bowl, lightly beat the remaining egg.
7. In a blender or food processor, combine the panko bread crumbs, lemon zest, and crushed red pepper flakes. Transfer the contents to a third bowl.
8. Take the large spoonfuls of the lump crab mixture and form them into golf ball sized fritters.
9. Dip each one first into the flour, then the egg, and finally the panko mixture.
10. Place them in the air fryer and cook for 10 minutes.
11. Serve with your favorite seafood dipping sauce.

Vegetables, Sides and Snacks
Classic French Fries

Serves: 6 - Cook Time: 25 minutes
Nutritional Information: Calories 176.7, Total Fat 3.6 g, Saturated Fat 0.6 g,
Total Carbohydrate 33.4 g, Dietary Fiber 5.1 g, Sugars 2.4 g, Protein 3.6 g

Ingredients:

2 pounds potatoes
1 tablespoon olive oil
1 teaspoon salt
1 teaspoon black pepper, coarsely ground

Directions:

1. Peel the potatoes, if desired, and cut them into thick matchstick-style strips.
2. Place the potatoes in cold water for approximately 30 minutes.
3. Remove the potatoes from the water and blot off any excess moisture.
4. Set the air fryer to 365°F.
5. Sprinkle the potatoes with olive oil and season them with salt and black pepper.
6. Place the potatoes in the basket of the air fryer.
7. Cook for 15 minutes, and then shake the basket to toss the potatoes. Increase the heat to 385°F and cook for an additional 10 minutes.
8. Remove the fries from the air fryer and serve with your favorite dipping sauce.

French Fry Style Zucchini

Serves: 4 - Cook Time: 15 minutes
Nutritional Information: Calories 58.8, Total Fat 3.6 g, Saturated Fat 0.5 g,
Total Carbohydrate 7.1 g, Dietary Fiber 2.5 g, Sugars 3.0 g, Protein 1.2 g

Ingredients:
1 ½ pounds zucchini
1 tablespoon olive oil
1 teaspoon salt
1 teaspoon black pepper
½ teaspoon old bay seasoning

Directions:
1. Set the air fryer to 390°F.
2. Peel the zucchini, if desired. Cut the zucchini in half widthwise and then cut into thick matchstick-style slices.
3. Coat the zucchini slices with olive oil.
4. Place the zucchini slices in the basket of the air fryer and cook for 12-15 minutes.
5. Remove the zucchini from the air fryer and season the fries with salt, black pepper, and old bay seasoning.

Five Spice Eggplant Fries

Serves: 4 - Cook Time: 15 minutes
Nutritional Information: Calories 137.8, Total Fat 10.7 g, Saturated Fat 1.5 g,
Total Carbohydrate 11.2 g, Dietary Fiber 3.5 g, Sugars 0.0 g, Protein 1.4 g

Ingredients:

1 eggplant, about 1 ½ pounds
1 ½ teaspoons salt
3 tablespoons olive oil
3 tablespoons cornstarch
1 teaspoon black pepper
1 teaspoon five spice powder

Directions:

1. Peel the eggplant and cut it in half widthwise. Slice the eggplant into thick matchstick-style slices.
2. Lay the eggplant out on a towel and sprinkle the slices with about half the salt. Let the slices sit for at least 5 minutes to allow the salt to pull out some of the excess moisture.
3. Lightly brush off the eggplant slices to remove the moisture and extra salt.
4. Set the air fryer to 390°F.
5. In a bowl, combine the remaining salt, olive oil, cornstarch, black pepper, and five spice powder. Mix well.
6. Toss the eggplant slices in the spiced olive oil mixture, coating them lightly with your hands as necessary.
7. Place the eggplant slices in the basket of the air fryer.
8. Cook for 12-15 minutes.

Root Vegetable Snack Chips

Serves: 6 - Cook Time: 20 minutes per batch
Nutritional Information: Calories 115.6, Total Fat 3.8 g, Saturated Fat 0.5 g,
Total Carbohydrate 19.9 g, Dietary Fiber 3.9 g, Sugars 5.1 g, Protein 1.8 g

Ingredients:
1 ½ cups beet, thinly sliced
1 ½ cups sweet potato, thinly sliced
1 ½ cups parsnip, thinly sliced
1 cup purple carrots, thinly sliced
1 ½ tablespoons olive oil
1 teaspoon salt
1 teaspoon black pepper
½ teaspoon cayenne powder
1 teaspoon chili powder
1 teaspoon brown sugar

Directions:
1. Set the air fryer to 420°F.
2. Place the sliced root vegetables in a bowl and drizzle them with the olive oil. Toss the vegetables to coat evenly.
3. Working in batches if necessary, place the vegetable chips in the basket of the air fryer and cook for 18-20 minutes.
4. While the chips are cooking, combine the salt, black pepper, cayenne powder, chili powder, and brown sugar.
5. Remove the root vegetables from the air fryer and immediately toss them with the seasoning mixture.

Mexican Roasted Baby Carrots

Serves: 4 - Cook Time: 20 minutes
Nutritional Information: Calories 65.0, Total Fat 3.5 g, Saturated Fat 0.5 g,
Total Carbohydrate 8.0 g, Dietary Fiber 2.0 g, Sugars 4.0 g, Protein 1.0 g

Ingredients:

4 cups baby carrots

1 tablespoon olive oil

1 teaspoon ground cumin

1 teaspoon Mexican oregano

½ teaspoon cayenne powder

1 teaspoon salt

1 teaspoon black pepper

¼ cup fresh cilantro

Directions:

1. Set the air fryer to 390°F.
2. Drizzle the carrots with the olive oil and season them with the ground cumin, Mexican oregano, cayenne powder, salt, and black pepper. Toss to mix.
3. Place the carrots in the air fryer and cook for 20 minutes.
4. Remove the carrots from the air fryer and toss them with the fresh cilantro before serving.

Brussels Sprouts with Balsamic Shallot Reduction

Serves: 4 - Cook Time: 20 minutes
Nutritional Information: Calories 111.7, Total Fat 6.1 g, Saturated Fat 1.9 g,
Total Carbohydrate 10.8 g, Dietary Fiber 3.0 g, Sugars 2.0 g, Protein 3.7 g

Ingredients:
4 cups Brussels sprouts
1 tablespoon olive oil
1 teaspoon salt
1 teaspoon black pepper, coarsely ground
2 teaspoons butter
½ cup pancetta, diced
¼ cup shallots, diced
¼ cup balsamic vinegar
1 sprig fresh rosemary

Directions:
1. Set the air fryer to 390°F.
2. Toss the Brussels sprouts with the olive oil, salt, and black pepper.
3. Place them in the air fryer and cook for 20 minutes.
4. While the Brussels sprouts are cooking, melt the butter in a skillet over medium heat.
5. Once the butter is melted, add the pancetta and the shallots. Cook, stirring frequently, until the pancetta is browned and the shallots are tender.
6. Pour the balsamic vinegar into the skillet and add the sprig of rosemary.
7. Bring the sauce to a boil, then reduce the heat and let it simmer until the liquid is reduced by about half.
8. Remove the Brussels sprouts from the air fryer and place them in a bowl.
9. Drizzle the balsamic reduction over them and toss to evenly season.
10. Serve immediately.

Sweet Potato Croquettes

Serves: 4 - Cook Time: 10 minutes
Nutritional Information: Calories 275.3, Total Fat 10.1 g, Saturated Fat 5.6 g,
Total Carbohydrate 33.6 g, Dietary Fiber 4.1 g, Sugars 9.4 g, Protein 12.7 g

Ingredients:

2 cups mashed sweet potatoes
½ cup freshly grated Asiago cheese
1 egg, plus 1 egg yolk
2 tablespoons flour, divided
1 tablespoon fresh thyme, chopped
½ teaspoon nutmeg
1 teaspoon salt
1 teaspoon black pepper
½ cup seasoned bread crumbs

Directions:

1. Set the air fryer to 390°F.
2. In a bowl, combine the mashed sweet potatoes, Asiago cheese, egg yolk, 1 tablespoon of the flour, thyme, nutmeg, salt, and black pepper.
3. Take heaping spoonfuls of the mixture and using your hands, form golf ball sized mounds.
4. Dust each one with the remaining flour.
5. Lightly beat the remaining egg and coat each croquette with it before rolling it in the seasoned bread crumbs.
6. Place the croquettes in the air fryer and cook, working in batches if necessary, for 8-9 minutes.
7. Remove the croquettes from the air fryer and serve with your favorite dipping sauce, if desired.

Roasted Caprese Stacks

Serves: 4 - Cook Time: 15 minutes
Nutritional Information: Calories 120.9, Total Fat 8.3 g, Saturated Fat 3.4 g,
Total Carbohydrate 5.0 g, Dietary Fiber 1.0 g, Sugars 0.0 g, Protein 7.6 g

Ingredients:

2 cups heirloom tomatoes, sliced thick
1 cup fresh mozzarella cheese, sliced thin
¼ cup fresh basil, chopped
1 teaspoon salt
1 teaspoon black pepper
2 tablespoons balsamic vinegar
1 tablespoon olive oil

Directions:

1. Set the air fryer to 390°F.
2. Begin by dividing the tomatoes into groups of three slices.
3. Place one tomato from each group onto a baking sheet.
4. Top each with a slice of mozzarella cheese, a drizzle of balsamic vinegar, and a sprinkling of salt and black pepper.
5. Top each with an additional piece of tomato.
6. Next, add on the remaining cheese, fresh basil, and any remaining balsamic vinegar, salt, and black pepper.
7. Top each with the last piece of tomato from each group.
8. Brush each stack lightly with olive oil.
9. Carefully place the stacks in the basket of the air fryer.
10. Cook for 12-15 minutes.

Individual Portabella White Pizzas

Serves: 4 - Cook Time: 5 minutes
Nutritional Information: Calories 229.9, Total Fat 19.3 g, Saturated Fat 7.9 g,
Total Carbohydrate 6.4 g, Dietary Fiber 3.5 g, Sugars 2.2 g, Protein 10.6 g

Ingredients:
4 large portabella mushroom caps
2 teaspoons olive oil
1 teaspoon salt
1 teaspoon black pepper, coarsely ground
½ teaspoon rubbed sage
¼ cup crème fraîche
1 tablespoon fresh chives, chopped
½ cup goat cheese, crumbled
½ cup fresh mozzarella cheese, shredded
¼ cup walnuts, chopped

Directions:
1. Set the air fryer to 325°F.
2. Brush the mushroom caps with olive oil and season them with salt, black pepper, and rubbed sage.
3. Combine the crème fraîche with the chives, and spread a layer on each mushroom cap.
4. Top each mushroom with goat cheese, mozzarella cheese, and walnuts.
5. Place the mushroom caps in the air fryer and cook for 5 minutes.

56

Dessert Recipes
Spiced Peach and Pistachio
Empanadas

Serves: 4 - Cook Time: 15 minutes
Nutritional Information: Calories 557.4 , Total Fat 24.7 g, Saturated Fat 10.0 g,
Total Carbohydrate 85.6 g, Dietary Fiber 7.6 g, Sugars 36.9 g, Protein 10.2 g

Ingredients:
3 cups peaches, diced
2 tablespoons butter, diced
¼ cup brown sugar
2 teaspoons cinnamon
½ teaspoon cayenne powder
1 teaspoon vanilla extract
1 tablespoon cornstarch
¼ cup orange juice
8-10 empanada shells
1 egg, lightly beaten
½ cup pistachios, chopped
½ cup dark chocolate pieces

Directions:
1. Melt the butter in a large skillet over medium heat.
2. When the butter has melted, add the peaches and season them with the brown sugar, cinnamon, cayenne powder, vanilla extract, and cornstarch. Cook for 5 minutes.
3. Add the orange juice and cook until the liquid bubbles. Reduce the heat and simmer until the peaches become tender and the resulting sauce thickens. Remove the skillet from the heat and set it aside.
4. Set the air fryer to 350°F.
5. Lay the empanada shells out on the counter or other flat surface.

6. Brush the edges with the lightly beaten egg.
7. Add the pistachios and chocolate pieces to the peach mixture.
8. Spoon the mixture onto one half of each of the empanada shells.
9. Fold the shell in half and crimp the edges to seal.
10. Lightly brush the empanadas with the beaten egg.
11. Place the empanadas in the air fryer basket and cook for 15 minutes.
12. Remove the empanadas from the air fryer and let them cool slightly before serving.

Walnut Raisin Stuffed Apples

Serves: 4 - Cook Time: 10 minutes
Nutritional Information: Calories 253.9, Total Fat 11.0 g, Saturated Fat 4.2 g,
Total Carbohydrate 45.0 g, Dietary Fiber 4.2 g, Sugars 37.3 g, Protein 1.9 g

Ingredients:

4 large apples
2 tablespoons butter, diced
¼ cup brown sugar
¼ cup walnuts, chopped
2 tablespoons raisins, chopped
1 tablespoon orange zest
1 tablespoon honey

Directions:

1. Set the air fryer to 350°F.
2. Slice the tops off of the apples and core each of them, leaving a generous well in the center.
3. Next, score the outside of each apple to allow additional steam to escape during cooking.
4. In a bowl, combine the butter, brown sugar, walnuts, raisins, and orange zest. Mix well.
5. Add an equal amount of the sweet mixture into the center of each apple.
6. Drizzle honey over the top of each apple and then replace the top part of the apple.
7. Place the apples in the air fryer and cook for 10-12 minutes, or until tender.

Lavender Honey Roasted Figs with Orange Scented Goat Cheese

Serves: 4 - Cook Time: 5 minutes
Nutritional Information: Calories 134.6, Total Fat 4.4 g, Saturated Fat 2.8 g,
Total Carbohydrate 23.0 g, Dietary Fiber 1.9 g, Sugars 20.7 g, Protein 1.7 g

Ingredients:

8 fresh figs
1 tablespoon butter, diced
3 tablespoons lavender honey
¼ cup goat cheese
1 teaspoon orange zest

Directions:

1. Set the air fryer to 350°F.
2. Take each fig and slice an x on one side. Gently pry it open just enough to insert a small amount of the diced butter.
3. Place the figs in an ovenproof dish, with the scored side up. Drizzle the honey over the figs and then place the dish in the air fryer and cook for 5-6 minutes.
4. While the figs are cooking, combine the goat cheese and orange zest.
5. Remove the figs from the air fryer, and gently open each one just enough to stuff it with a small spoonful of the goat cheese mixture.
6. Drizzle with more honey, if desired, before serving.

Papaya Ginger Flan

Serves: 4 - Cook Time: 40 minutes
Nutritional Information: Calories 241.4, Total Fat 5.7 g, Saturated Fat 2.8 g,
Total Carbohydrate 42.0 g, Dietary Fiber 0.1 g, Sugars 41.5 g, Protein 6.5 g

Ingredients:

½ cup white sugar
1 teaspoon fresh ginger, grated
1 tablespoon water
¼ cup evaporated milk
¼ cup sweetened condensed milk
¼ cup papaya nectar
½ cup coconut milk
2 eggs, plus 1 egg yolk
1 cup fresh papaya, sliced
1 tablespoon fresh mint, chopped
1 teaspoon lime juice

Directions:

1. Set the air fryer to 325°F and pour 2 cups of hot water into the bottom.
2. In a saucepan, combine the white sugar, ginger, and water over medium to medium-high heat. Cook, stirring frequently, until a golden caramel sauce is formed.
3. Lightly oil four individual serving size ramekins.
4. Pour equal amounts of the ginger caramel sauce into each of the ramekins.
5. In a bowl, combine the evaporated milk, sweetened condensed milk, papaya nectar, coconut milk, egg, and egg yolk.
6. Pour the custard mixture into each of the ramekins.
7. Place the ramekins in the air fryer and cook for 30 minutes.

8. Remove the ramekins, cover, and place them in the refrigerator for at least 2 hours, until ready to serve.
9. Before serving, sprinkle the papaya with lime juice and fresh mint. Garnish each ramekin with the papaya or serve it on the side.

Double Chocolate Brownies

Serves: 8 - Cook Time: 25 minutes
Nutritional Information: Calories 325.9, Total Fat 18.0 g, Saturated Fat 11.1 g,
Total Carbohydrate 43.0 g, Dietary Fiber 3.0 g, Sugars 32.2 g, Protein 3.5 g

Ingredients:
½ cup flour
½ cup dark unsweetened cocoa powder
2 teaspoons cinnamon
¼ teaspoon ground ginger
¼ teaspoon baking powder
¼ teaspoon salt
2 eggs
½ cup unsalted butter, softened
1 cup white sugar
1 teaspoon pure vanilla extract
½ cup chocolate chips

Directions:
1. Set the air fryer to 340°F.
2. Lightly oil a baking pan fitted to the air fryer.
3. In one bowl, combine the flour, dark unsweetened cocoa powder, cinnamon, ground ginger, baking powder, and salt.
4. In another bowl, mix together the eggs, butter, sugar, and vanilla extract.
5. Slowly, add the dry ingredients to the wet ingredients and mix.
6. Fold the chocolate chips into the brownie batter.
7. Spread the batter in the prepared pan.
8. Place the pan in the air fryer and cook for 20-25 minutes, or until set in the center.

Conclusion

Have you recently made a resolution to be healthier, or are you looking for a way to add a little diversity and excitement to your already healthy dietary lifestyle? These are two of the main reasons culinary enthusiasts are flocking to the air fryer, and they are experiencing great results. The air fryer is so much more than just a way to enjoy some typically unhealthy foods without all the guilt. It is an appliance that that can cook an incredible variety of dishes, including many that you probably never thought possible. The recipes in this book have been designed to give you a glimpse into the limitless potential of your air fryer. Once you see how simple it is to create healthy and delicious foods with your air fryer, there will be no question that the two of you will have a long, beautiful, healthy relationship. Enjoy your air fryer and use it every day. The possibilities are endless.

About the Author

Louise Davidson is an avid cook who likes simple flavors and easy-to-make meals. She lives in Tennessee with her husband, her three grown children, her two dogs, and the family's cat, Whiskers. She loves the outdoor and has mastered the art of camp cooking on open fires and barbecue grills.

In colder months, she loves to whip up some slow cooker meals, and uses her favorite cooking tools in her kitchen, the cast iron pans, and Dutch oven. She also is very busy preparing Christmas treats for her extended family and friends. She gets busy baking for the holiday season sometimes as early as October. Her recipes are cherished by everyone who has tasted her foods and holiday treats.

Louise is a part-time writer of cookbooks, sharing her love of food, her experience, and her family's secret recipes with her readers.

She also loves to learn and share tips and tricks to make life a breeze.

More Books from Louise Davidson

Appendix – Cooking Conversion Charts

1. Measuring Equivalent Chart

Type	Imperial	Imperial	Metric
Weight	1 dry ounce		28g
	1 pound	16 dry ounces	0.45 kg
Volume	1 teaspoon		5 ml
	1 dessert spoon	2 teaspoons	10 ml
	1 tablespoon	3 teaspoons	15 ml
	1 Australian tablespoon	4 teaspoons	20 ml
	1 fluid ounce	2 tablespoons	30 ml
	1 cup	16 tablespoons	240 ml
	1 cup	8 fluid ounces	240 ml
	1 pint	2 cups	470 ml
	1 quart	2 pints	0.95 l
	1 gallon	4 quarts	3.8 l
Length	1 inch		2.54 cm

* Numbers are rounded to the closest equivalent

2. Oven Temperature Equivalent Chart

T(°F)	T(°C)
220	100
225	110
250	120
275	140
300	150
325	160
350	180
375	190
400	200
425	220
450	230
475	250
500	260

* $T(°C) = [T(°F)-32] * 5/9$
** $T(°F) = T(°C) * 9/5 + 32$
*** Numbers are rounded to the closest equivalent

Printed in Great Britain
by Amazon